SOLVING MYSTERIES WITH SCIENCE

ALIENS AND UFOs

LORI HILE

Raintree
Chicago, Illinois

Edited by Adam Miller, Vaarunika Dharmapala, and
Claire Throp
Designed by Ken Vail Graphic Design
Original illustrations © Capstone Global Library Ltd
2014
Illustrated by Chris King
Picture research by Mica Brancic
Production by Victoria Fitzgerald
Originated by Capstone Global Library Ltd

**Library of Congress Cataloging-in-Publication
Data**
Hile, Lori.

  Aliens & UFOs / Lori Hile.—1st ed.
    p. cm.—(Solving mysteries with science)
  Includes bibliographical references and index.
  Summary: "More than any other strange
phenomena, the existence of life on other planets has
sparked the most discussion. Many have claimed to
have seen strange spacecraft and some are absolutely
sure they've been abducted by aliens. Is there any
truth to these stories? Could life "out there" exist?
Using the scientific method and other information,
this book aims to find out!"—Provided by publisher.
  ISBN 978-1-4109-5498-5 (hb)—ISBN 978-1-4109-
5504-3 (pb)
  1. Unidentified flying objects—Juvenile literature. 2.
Extraterrestrial beings—Juvenile literature. I. Title. II.
Title: Aliens and UFOs. III. Series: Solving mysteries
with science.

TL789.2.H55 2014
001.942—dc23   2012042236

Acknowledgments
We would like to thank the following for permission to
reproduce photographs: Alamy pp. 27 (© AF archive),
31 (© Mary Evans Picture Library), 18 bottom
(© World History Archive), 21 top (© Thierry Grun);
AP/Press Association Images p. 32 (Susan Walsh);
Corbis p. 26 (© Bettmann); Dreamstime p. 33
(Innovari); Fortean Photo Library p. (18 top); Getty
Images pp. 4 to 5 (Blend Images/PBNJ Productions),
20 to 21 (Science Photo Library/Magrath/Folsom),
22 (Purestock), 23 (AFP Photo/Fabrice Coffrini),
25 (Dave M. Benett), 35 (Visuals Unlimited, Inc./
Victor Habbick), 36 (Science Photo Library/Laguna
Design), 43 (Photographer's Choice RF/Siede
Preis); NASA p. 34 to 35 (Spitzer Space Telescope
Collection); Photographer unknown p. 29; Reuters
p. 37 (© Scanpix Norway/Anita Olsen); Shutterstock
pp. 5, 19 (© Albert Ziganshin), 24 to 25 (© Daniele
Carotenuto), 28 to 29 (© Bairachnyi Dmitry), 32 to
33 (© revolution), 37 (frenta/© Lukiyanova Natalia),
40 (© Vlue), 40 to 41 (© photobank.kiev.ua), 42
(© photoBeard); 29; The Kobal Collection pp. 38
(Universal/Amblin), 39 (Universal), 41 (Battleship
Delta Productions).

Background design images supplied by Shutterstock
(©Zuzuan), (© argus), (© Vitaly Korovin).

Cover photograph of a UFO hovering over a winter
scene reproduced with permission of Getty Images
(Visuals Unlimited, Inc./Victor Habbick).

Every effort has been made to contact copyright
holders of material reproduced in this book. Any
omissions will be rectified in subsequent printings if
notice is given to the publisher.

Printed in the United States   5073

CONTENTS

UP IN THE AIR

Is it a bird? A plane? Have you ever looked up at the sky and seen something you didn't recognize? Something that looks and behaves differently than birds, airplanes, stars, planets, or clouds? Then you might have witnessed a UFO, or Unidentified Flying Object! For centuries, people have noticed odd objects in the sky, but only in the last century have many of these sightings been carefully recorded.

Some people also claim to have seen strange creatures on board these unidentified objects. Often these creatures look a lot like humans, only with different colored skin, bigger eyes or heads, fewer fingers, or shorter, thinner bodies. Because they are unlike ordinary humans, these creatures are called "extraterrestrials" (ETs) or aliens and are believed by many to be visitors from outer space.

But what do we really know about UFOs and aliens? Do they truly exist? And, if so, are they really from outer space? In the first part of this book, you will read dramatic, real-life accounts from people who have witnessed odd, unidentified objects in the sky. Some of them have even described encounters with aliens. The second part of the book uses science to examine exactly what it is that so many people have reported seeing.

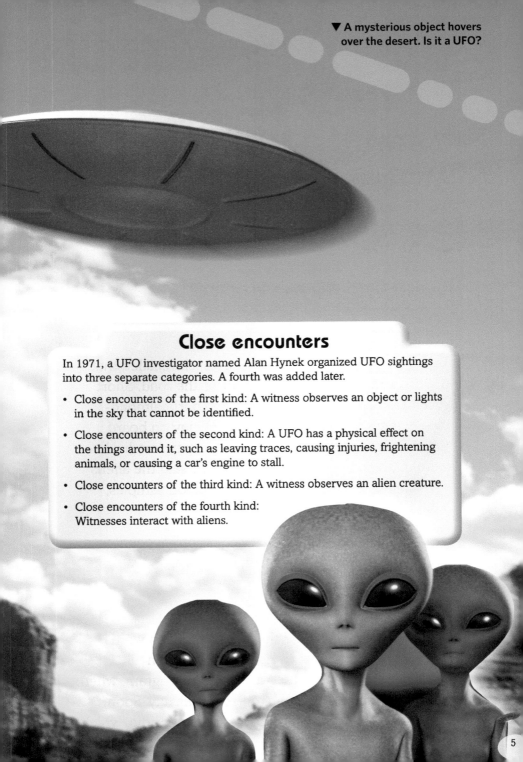

Close encounters

In 1971, a UFO investigator named Alan Hynek organized UFO sightings into three separate categories. A fourth was added later.

- Close encounters of the first kind: A witness observes an object or lights in the sky that cannot be identified.

- Close encounters of the second kind: A UFO has a physical effect on the things around it, such as leaving traces, causing injuries, frightening animals, or causing a car's engine to stall.

- Close encounters of the third kind: A witness observes an alien creature.

- Close encounters of the fourth kind: Witnesses interact with aliens.

CLOSE ENCOUNTERS OF THE FIRST, SECOND, AND THIRD KIND

Pilot and businessman Kenneth Arnold soared through the clear blue skies over Washington state's Cascade Mountains in his small airplane. It was June 1947, and Arnold was searching for the remains of an airplane that had recently crashed. Suddenly, his search was interrupted by a blinding flash of light! Arnold peered out of the window, but all he could see was a distant airplane.

Soon, another series of flashes caught his eye. When Arnold looked out, he was startled by what he saw. Nine peculiar-looking aircraft were flying in formation over the tops of the mountains! These wingless metallic objects were unlike anything Arnold had ever seen before.

FASTER THAN A JET

They were moving so quickly that Arnold decided to calculate their speed. According to his estimates, they were moving at 1,700 miles (2,735 kilometers) per hour, three times faster than any airplane could travel in 1947—and twice the speed of sound!

Arnold opened the window to make sure the objects were not simply reflections. But he could still see the objects "skipping like saucers through the air."

BIRTH OF THE FLYING SAUCER

When Arnold landed, he reported his sighting to the airport manager. The next day, a newspaper reporter interviewed Arnold and published an article announcing Arnold's "flying saucers." Although people had viewed strange flying objects before, Arnold's sighting was one of the first official UFO reports. Afterward, many people came forward with their own UFO stories.

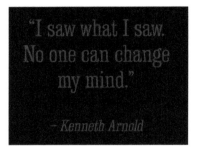

"I saw what I saw. No one can change my mind."

– Kenneth Arnold

A BRIGHT OBJECT

On September 19, 1976, puzzled residents called the Iranian Air Force command center in Tehran, Iran, reporting a strange, bright object in the sky. Some people said it looked like "a helicopter with a shining light." The officer on duty knew that no helicopters were in the area, so he told the residents they must be seeing a star. But after workers at the control tower reported the same object, he decided to look for himself. The object shone like a star, but it was bigger and brighter than the Sun! And it appeared to be moving. Worried that it might be a secret enemy weapon, the officer ordered an F-4 fighter plane to investigate.

CHASING A UFO

The fighter jet climbed swiftly, but when it reached within 25 miles (40 kilometers) of the brilliant light, its communications devices and instrument panel suddenly failed! As soon as the pilot turned away from the UFO, the jet regained communication and instrumentation.

Soon, another F-4 jet was sent up to identify the UFO. But when the second plane got within 25 miles (40 kilometers) of the light, the UFO sped up. The F-4 was flying faster than the speed of sound, but it still couldn't catch up with the UFO! The pilot tried to get a good look at the object, but all he could see were bright, multicolored lights that rotated so quickly that they blurred together.

FAILURE TO LAUNCH

Then, suddenly, a smaller light broke away from the UFO and headed directly for the jet! Believing he was in danger, the pilot aimed a missile at the object. But just as he was about to fire, his weapons control panel and communications devices shut down! The pilot turned sharply to avoid the UFO, but it continued to follow him. Then it sped up and rejoined the larger UFO, which soared away at four times the speed of sound.

A GLOWING PYRAMID

A staff sergeant shook security officer James Penniston awake shortly after midnight on December 26, 1980, and informed him that an aircraft may have crashed at Rendlesham Forest, near Bentwaters Air Force Base in England.

When Penniston and two airmen arrived at the forest, they encountered an object glowing so brightly that Penniston had to squint. It was shaped like a pyramid, about 9 feet (2.7 meters) wide and 6½ feet (2 meters) tall, with swirling blue and yellow lights. The air around them felt electrically charged, and their radios crackled. Penniston touched the craft's surface, which was carved with picture-like symbols. It looked metallic, yet it felt warm and smooth, like fabric.

IMPOSSIBLE SPEED

Penniston snapped photos and took notes for an hour, before the object grew brighter and lifted silently off the ground. Once it cleared the trees, it shot off so fast that Penniston wrote in his log book: "Speed: <u>Impossible!</u>"

IT'S BACK!

"It's back!" a security patrol lieutenant announced two nights later, at the base's Christmas party. This time the deputy base-commander, Chuck Halt, and his crew were greeted by an object in the forest that glowed like the Sun, with a dark spot in the center, like the pupil of an eye.

Soon, the object soared above the trees and exploded into five pieces. The objects moved in formation, at right angles, then rushed together, forming a laser-like beam that shone down to the ground. Then the objects vanished into the night.

> "I do know one thing, without a doubt. These objects were under intelligent control."
>
> – Colonel Halt

Fire at Falcon Lake

Mechanic Stephen Michalak planned a relaxing vacation at Falcon Lake, Canada, in 1967. But on his second day, he saw two huge, glowing disc-shaped objects descending from the sky! One hovered, while the other landed only 150 feet (45 meters) away, flashing red, orange, and gray lights.

As a door opened on the side of the craft, Michalak could see bright lights and hear voices. He touched the craft, which melted his glove! Then, suddenly, the UFO moved, leaving a trail of air so hot it set fire to Michalak's clothes. He ripped off his shirt just as the craft lifted off.

Afterward, Michalak had a stomachache and a severe headache. Later, he would suffer symptoms of radiation poisoning and find a mysterious grill mark on his stomach (see page 31).

BIZARRE BLACK DUST

Late one night in January 1988, Sean Knowles was driving his mother, two brothers, and two dogs down a lonely stretch of road on their way to Melbourne, Australia, when the radio suddenly failed. A few minutes later, Knowles spotted a strange ball of light floating in front of their car. Shaped like a giant egg in a cup, the object was just under 3 feet (1 meter) wide, with a golden center.

Sean sped up, but it was too late. Thump. The object landed on top of the car! Then it sucked the car several feet up off the road! Sean's mother, Faye, stretched her arm out the window to touch the object, which felt warm and spongy. When she pulled her hand back in, it was caked in a strange black dust. The dogs started barking, and the family members felt like they were talking in slow motion.

Then, suddenly, the car slammed back to the road, bursting a tire. By the time the family reached the nearest gas station—25 miles (40 kilometers) away—Faye's hand had started to swell, and the dogs had begun losing clumps of hair. Shaken, the Knowles family reported the scary story to the gas station attendant, who told them a truck driver had seen a similar light.

ALIEN ENCOUNTERS AND ABDUCTIONS

BETTY AND BARNEY HILL

Late one night in September 1961, Barney Hill and his wife, Betty, were driving home through the White Mountains in New Hampshire, when they noticed a bright light keeping pace with their car. At first, they thought it might be a satellite or airplane, but when Betty peeked through binoculars, she spotted colored lights and a circular row of windows. Barney pulled over, and through binoculars he could see small figures in dark uniforms peering out the windows! He rushed Betty back to the car, convinced that the creatures were going to capture them.

MISSING TIME

As the Hills sped off, they heard an odd beeping sound and felt a tingling sensation. Before they knew it, two hours had passed, and they were 35 miles (56 kilometers) farther down the road. Both of them felt that something strange had happened, but neither of them knew exactly what it was.

At home, Betty noticed that her dress was stained and that both of their watches had stopped working. Betty also started having nightmares that she had been taken on board a UFO. Barney developed a rash and an ulcer. At their doctor's suggestion, the couple consulted a hypnotist.

TAKEN ABOARD

Under hypnosis, Betty and Barney each recalled that the UFO had landed in the center of the road. Short creatures with large, bald heads and dark, almond-shaped eyes had taken Betty and Barney on board the craft, undressed them, and given them medical examinations in separate rooms. They said the aliens took skin scrapings, saliva samples, blood samples, locks of hair, and nail clippings.

Betty and Barney Hill's "alien abduction" account was one of the first to become widely known.

FAMILY ABDUCTION!

John and Susan Day and their three children were hurrying to their home in Essex, England, on October 27, 1974, to watch a television program, when they saw a blue egg-shaped object in the sky. Soon, everything went silent except for their car radio, which began to crackle. As a green mist enveloped the car, the headlights stopped working and the car lurched, like someone else was steering it. Moments later, the car jolted, as if it hit a bump. The mist vanished, and the Days found themselves further down the road.

When they arrived home, the Days settled in to watch their television program. But it was already over. When they checked the clock, they discovered the time was almost three hours later than it should have been!

CHANGES

After the experience, all of the Days began behaving differently. Susan and John both stopped eating meat and drinking alcohol, and John stopped smoking. Their son, Kevin, who had been a struggling reader, began devouring books at a level way beyond his years. And all of them began to fight pollution.

WE ARE ALWAYS HERE

Under hypnosis sessions a few years later, both Susan and John recalled being taken by tall aliens on board a "craft" and being examined. While there, they were shown hundreds of maps, charts, photos, and drawings, including a holographic image of Earth destroyed by pollution. The Days, who were able to communicate telepathically with the aliens, asked if the aliens were visiting from another planet. The aliens said they were not visiting, because they were "always here."

Flying eggs? Portrait of a UFO

UFOs come in all shapes and sizes, but most UFOs appear to have some of the following features in common.

- They are shaped like a cigar, cylinder, egg, or saucer.
- They make sharp turns at angles impossible for known technology.
- They move at supersonic speeds.
- They fly quietly or silently.
- They affect technology.

INVESTIGATING UFOS AND ALIENS

Thousands of years ago, a man looked to the skies and saw a huge cloud surrounded by a brilliant light. On it were four creatures with shiny bronze feet. This vision was recorded in the Bible's book of Ezekiel, written around 569 BCE. Throughout the ages, people in every part of the world have reported strange visions in the skies. An ancient Egyptian scroll from 11,000 BCE tells of a group of residents who threw themselves to the ground in fear after witnessing a mass of fiery objects swarm the skies.

In Nazca, Peru, a plateau of about 193 square miles (500 square kilometers) contains strange animal images and geometrical patterns that can only be seen from high in the sky. No one knows exactly who created these pictures or why. Could they have been inspired or created by aliens? Many early cultures tell stories of wise beings descending from the sky to teach humans.

▲ Between 1561 and 1566, residents of Nuremberg, Germany, reported seeing strange spheres, discs, and tubes battle each other in the sky, as shown in this woodcut.

◀ Based on a description in the Bible's book of Ezekiel, a NASA engineer built a flying machine that actually worked.

Fact or fiction?

What have all of these witnesses seen? Are they imagining things? Are they exaggerating their stories? Are some of them lying? Many people believe that UFOs are vehicles from outer space inhabited by alien creatures. But others believe that UFOs have more "down to earth" explanations. This section of the book uses the scientific method to investigate the mystery of UFOs and aliens.

The scientific method

Good investigators follow the scientific method when they need to establish and test a theory. The scientific method has five basic steps:

1. Make observations (comments based on studying something closely).
2. Do some background research.
3. Form a testable hypothesis. This is basically a prediction, or "educated guess," to explain the observations.
4. Conduct experiments or find evidence to support the hypothesis.
5. After thinking carefully about the evidence, draw conclusions.

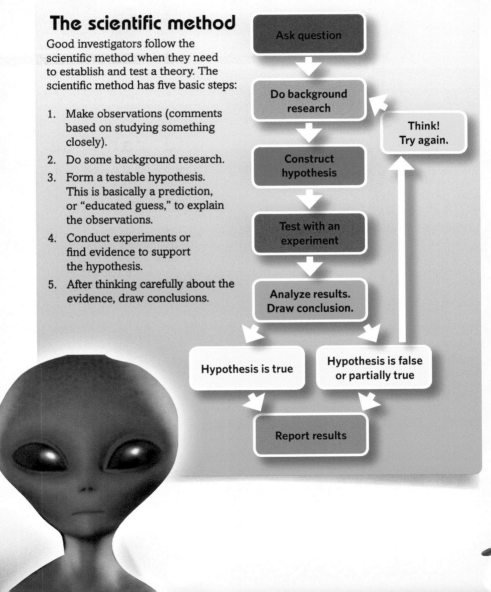

Ask question

Do background research

Think! Try again.

Construct hypothesis

Test with an experiment

Analyze results. Draw conclusion.

Hypothesis is true

Hypothesis is false or partially true

Report results

UFO OR IFO?

Most people who report UFOs are not seeing UFOs at all! Government records show that from 75 to 90 percent of UFO sightings turn out to be ordinary objects. This makes them IFOs (Identified Flying Objects), not UFOs. The following natural objects are sometimes mistaken for UFOs.

Pelican theory

Remember the nine metallic objects that pilot Kenneth Arnold saw flying in formation (see page 6)? Researcher James Easton believes that Arnold's "flying saucers" were actually flying pelicans! Some people find this explanation absurd, but when birds fly at high altitudes, the Sun can reflect off their oily feathers, making them glisten like metal. Pelicans also fly in formation, and their wingspan can reach almost 9 feet (2.7 meters)!

The Venus trap

In April 1966, two American police officers drove through two states in pursuit of a bright, disc-shaped object. Government investigators concluded that the men had been chasing Venus, an unusually bright planet that was rising at the time. There is a rise in UFO reports whenever Venus is especially bright in the sky.

Great balls of fire!

It's a dark and stormy night. Boom! The thunder echoes, and several giant globes of fire float down from the sky, whirling over bushes and bouncing off the ground before exploding like cannons. For years, people have reported seeing strange fireballs like these, but scientists have doubted their accounts. Recently, these fiery spheres—made from electricity—have been given a name: ball lightning. Because this form of lightning is rare, it could be mistaken for a UFO.

Lenticular clouds

In December 1953, airplane engineer Kelly Johnson observed a long, dark object with blurred edges hovering over his ranch in California. A U.S. Air Force investigator said that Johnson's UFO was probably just a lenticular cloud. Even though Johnson doubts this explanation, this type of lens-shaped cloud formation has fooled many.

◄ Lenticular (lens-shaped) clouds, which sometimes form at high altitudes, can resemble a "flying saucer," especially when they reflect the Sun's glow.

Made on Earth

Some human-made objects can also be blamed for UFO sightings.

Up, up, and away: Weather balloons

Every day, meteorologists release over 800 weather balloons into the sky. These teardrop-shaped balloons relay weather conditions back to Earth with a device dangling from their strings. But they are often mistaken for UFOs, since they look so different than normal balloons. They can expand as wide as a bus, and when they reflect sunlight, they can cast an eerie glow.

Night lights

Every evening for several weeks, a Frenchman saw odd flashing lights on the clouds over his home. Investigators eventually discovered these were simply car headlights on a nearby mountain road, reflecting off the clouds. Other lights sometimes mistaken for UFOs include search lights, street lights, flares, and houselights. Lighthouse beams were given as one explanation for the Rendlesham Forest sighting (see page 10), although it does not fit with all of the facts.

Planes, helicopters, and other flying machines

While traditional airplanes are usually easy to recognize, many people are fooled by less common flying machines, such as helicopters, airplanes towing banners, fighter planes, blimps, or satellites.

Even more people are fooled by experimental military aircraft, which are sometimes triangle-shaped or even saucer-shaped. Although they usually fly high in the sky or in military air space, they are sometimes spotted elsewhere. Because the aircraft are top secret, the military often denies their existence, leading witnesses to conclude they are UFOs.

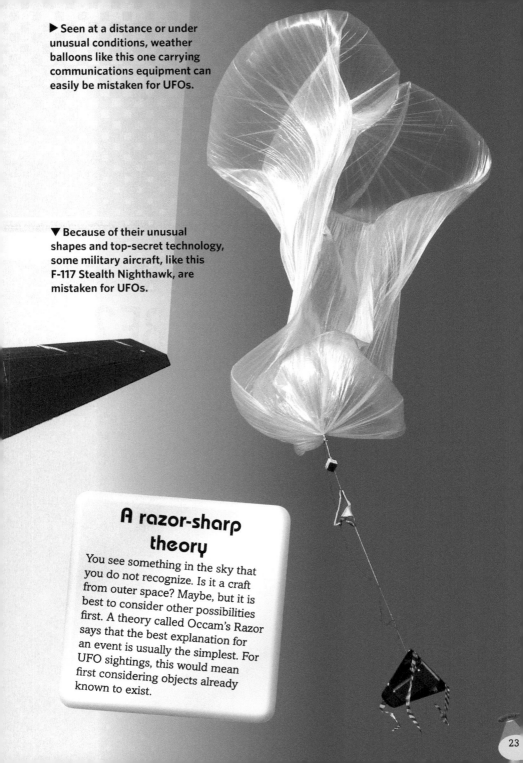

▶ Seen at a distance or under unusual conditions, weather balloons like this one carrying communications equipment can easily be mistaken for UFOs.

▼ Because of their unusual shapes and top-secret technology, some military aircraft, like this F-117 Stealth Nighthawk, are mistaken for UFOs.

A razor-sharp theory

You see something in the sky that you do not recognize. Is it a craft from outer space? Maybe, but it is best to consider other possibilities first. A theory called Occam's Razor says that the best explanation for an event is usually the simplest. For UFO sightings, this would mean first considering objects already known to exist.

UFO HOAXES

Many UFO sightings are cases of mistaken identity. But a small number—about 5 percent—are the result of deliberate hoaxes.

The alien autopsy film

In 1996, a British music and movie producer named Ray Santilli released shocking footage showing two doctors removing organs from the body of what looked like a dead alien. Santilli claimed his grainy, 17-minute black-and-white film was recorded in 1947, after a flying saucer had crashed in Roswell, New Mexico, and killed several aliens. Later in 1996, the Fox television network broadcast the footage in a program called *Alien Autopsy: Fact or Fiction?*. Several experts warned Fox that the footage was almost certainly fake, but the network broadcast the program anyway, knowing it would attract lots of viewers.

The program not only generated viewers, but it also generated a debate that raged for years. Believers pointed out that all of the details in the film seemed genuine for 1947, while skeptics (doubters) claimed that the film could easily be faked using computer graphics. Finally, in 2006, Santilli admitted that he had created most of the footage himself, even getting a homeless man to portray the film's original "photographer."

▶ Gary Shoefield (left) and Ray Santilli were both involved in making the alien autopsy footage.

No joke!

Many people behind hoaxes think they are playing harmless "pranks," but hoaxes are no laughing matter, especially when the media or authorities get involved. Because hoaxes are covered by the media, they can lead people to believe all UFO sightings are fake. Hoaxes also keep authorities away from investigating real UFO sightings or even crimes. They cloud UFO files with false information. Some people who played pranks have been arrested.

Billy Meier: Contactee or liar?

In 1979, a Swiss farmer named Billy Meier made an incredible claim. He said he had been communicating for years with a group of beautiful extraterrestrials called Pleiadians from the star cluster Pleiades. And he even provided incredibly clear and crisp photos and films of the ETs and their spaceships, in addition to notebooks filled with Pleiadian wisdom.

But not everyone was convinced. Researchers sped up his films and discovered that his "flying saucers" swung like pendulums, as if they were models attached to strings. Strings are also visible in some of Meier's photographs. And the lovely "Pleiadians" in his photos were identified as dancers from a U.S. television program.

Meier claims that his original photos were altered. But most serious UFO researchers have little doubt that Billy Meier is a fraud.

Men in black: Fact or fraud?

UFO investigator Albert Bender was at his home in Connecticut in 1954 when he was visited by three pale men dressed in black suits and hats. They told him to stop his UFO investigations immediately.

Since the 1950s, hundreds of people have reported similar visits shortly after witnessing or researching UFOs. Who are these mysterious men in black (MIB)?

Some people believe the MIB are government agents trying to gather and keep UFO information for themselves. Others believe that the MIB are aliens—or robots they have created—trying to scare people into keeping their presence a secret. Others suggest that witnesses are suffering hallucinations after stressful UFO encounters. Nick Pope, a former UFO investigator, believes that MIB are simply people creating hoaxes. Of course, it is also possible that witnesses are lying. MIB sightings have decreased in recent years, but the mystery remains.

▲ The *Men in Black* movies, starring Tommy Lee Jones (left) and Will Smith (right), were based on reports by UFO witnesses of visits by mysterious men wearing black suits.

THE EVIDENCE

Proven hoaxes and cases of mistaken identity account for most UFO reports. But up to one-fifth of sightings remain unexplained. Are these truly UFOs? Let's examine the evidence!

Mariana mystery

In August 1950, Nick Mariana, the owner of a minor league baseball team in Great Falls, Montana, climbed to the top of his stadium to check weather conditions before a game. That is when he noticed two bright, silvery discs spinning slowly overhead. Mariana grabbed a camera and filmed the mysterious objects.

The U.S. Air Force examined his film and claimed that the objects were shadows of fighter jets. But Mariana says that he saw fighter jets himself...after the discs had disappeared. Since then, many others have analyzed the film. Most believe it is genuine, partly because it was difficult to fake films in the 1950s, before computers were widely used. Most agree that the objects are not fighter jets. But it is impossible to prove exactly what they are...except UFOs.

▼ Bright lights in the sky have often been photographed, but never fully explained.

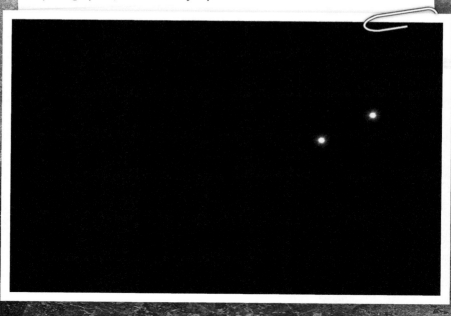

Belgian triangle photo

Between November 1989 and April 1990, thousands of people watched as flat, triangle-shaped objects with twinkling lights lit up the skies over Belgium. Despite so many sightings, only one clear photo surfaced, snapped by a young man named Patrick M. The photo was examined by many researchers, including NASA scientists. Most believed it was genuine. But in July 2011, Patrick M. confessed that he had faked the photo, using a model.

The fake photo does not disprove the Belgian triangles, but it does show why photos alone cannot prove sightings either. Photos are easy to fake using models or computers, and fakes can be difficult to detect. Also, UFOs are hard to capture on camera in the first place. Scientists believe the Belgian triangle gave off infrared light, which appears blurry on film.

▼ The best photo snapped of the "Belgian triangles" turned out to be a fake.

Radar, radiation, and rabbits

While it is difficult to find physical evidence for UFOs, such as an alien body or a crashed spaceship, we can examine marks or effects caused by UFOs.

Radar returns

On July 19, 1952, witnesses watched orange, glowing objects zigzag over Washington, D.C. Radar at two nearby airports also detected several unknown objects flying at high speeds. Radar has supported 74 other eyewitness UFO accounts, too, including the Belgian triangles (see page 29) and the Tehran UFO (see page 8). Radar errors are possible but highly unlikely when UFOs have also been spotted.

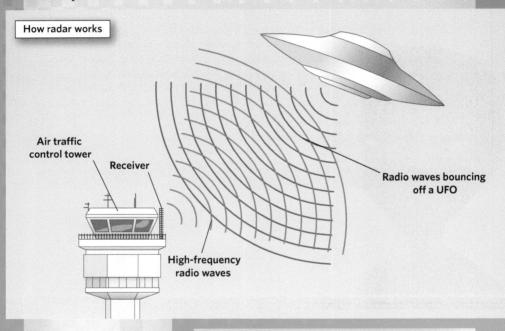

How radar works

Air traffic control tower

Receiver

Radio waves bouncing off a UFO

High-frequency radio waves

▲ To detect the presence, speed, distance, and direction of large objects in the sky, scientists send out high-frequency electromagnetic waves. Scientists can determine how far away an object is by how long it takes for the waves to bounce back.

Electromagnetic effects

We have read about cars, radios, and other electronic equipment failing when UFOs are near. Skeptics say that these devices may simply be old or outdated. Others say that witnesses under stress may accidentally turn off their cars or radios or misreport events. But scientists have also measured unusually strong electromagnetic fields, a force that can cause equipment failures, around some cars involved in UFO sightings.

Landing traces

There are 5,000 documented cases from 70 countries where UFOs have left burn marks, imprints, rings, and radiation. Investigators at Rendlesham Forest (see page 10) found three 7-inch (18-centimeter) indentations at the landing site—signs of a heavy object—and radiation levels eight times higher than normal. One skeptic claimed these markings were caused by rabbits. But as one investigator pointed out, there are very few 1.8-ton, radioactive rabbits!

Medical effects

After their UFO encounters, both Stephen Michalak (see page 12) and Faye Knowles (see page 13) became sick. When researchers examined the black dust left on Knowles's car, they found traces of the radioactive chemical astatine, which can cause radiation sickness. There are 400 other cases of UFO-related illnesses or injuries and 150 cases of UFO-related healings. However, it is difficult to prove these medical effects are a result of UFO contact.

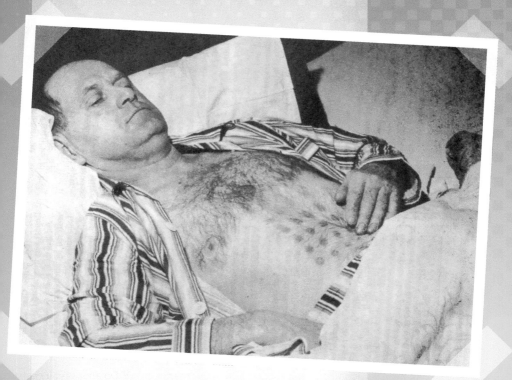

▲ After reporting a close encounter with a UFO, Canadian resident Stephen Michalak developed symptoms of radiation poisoning and a mysterious grill mark on his stomach.

Do my eyes deceive me?

What about eyewitnesses? Can we trust their extraordinary stories? Many abductees only recall their alien abduction experiences during a relaxation technique called hypnosis. Since hypnosis patients are relaxed, they are also very open to ideas and suggestions. So, if a hypnotist mentions an image or event, a patient might believe that image or event is part of his or her own memory. For example, one abductee undergoing hypnosis could not remember what happened after a UFO approached her car. But when a hypnotist showed her a picture of an "alien," she immediately "remembered" seeing an alien. Scientists worry that abductees' stories are filled with these types of "false memories."

Sincere and well-balanced

Many people believe that abductees are mentally ill or seeking attention. But John Mack, a psychiatrist at Harvard University, worked with hundreds of abductees and became convinced that most were sincere and mentally balanced. Lie detector tests, which are about 86 percent accurate, confirm that they are rarely lying. Psychologist Elizabeth Slater conducted psychological tests on UFO witnesses. She was surprised to find that they were healthier than all the other groups she had tested.

▶ Dr. John Mack believes that abductees are often telling the truth.

Memory test

Professor Alvin H. Lawson put a random group of people under hypnosis and asked them to imagine a UFO abduction experience. Their stories were very similar to those of abductees—with one big difference. Only the real abductees experienced fear and sadness while recounting their stories. This made it clear that the abductees had actually experienced some sort of trauma, unlike the people with the imagined experiences.

Alien implants and surgeries

Many abductees claim that aliens have implanted objects in their bodies, and some of these objects have been analyzed. All were made from earthly materials. However, Dr. Mack did observe fresh cuts and scars on the bodies of some abductees.

▲ Many abductees claim that aliens have performed surgery or medical experiments on them.

WHAT COULD IT BE?

Evidence suggests that a small percentage of UFOs are truly unknown objects. Some scientists believe that, given enough time, we will find common explanations for these unexplained objects. But these UFOs often look and act very differently than IFOs. They are usually brighter, faster, and more colorful. And the sightings frequently last longer and involve several objects. So, what could these objects be?

The ET hypothesis

When UFOs were first reported, few people believed they were alien spaceships, since space travel seemed impossible. Since then, humans have made giant leaps in space technology. Now over 99 percent of people who believe in UFOs believe the Extraterrestrial Hypothesis, which says that UFOs are spacecraft powered by ETs from other planets. But is this possible?

Are we alone?

Scientists estimate that there are 300 sextillion stars in the universe. That is a three followed by 23 zeros (300,000,000,000,000,000,000,000). That's a lot of stars! And many of these stars have planets orbiting them. Given these mind-blowing numbers, most scientists believe the odds are pretty good that intelligent life forms exist on other planets. But could those intelligent beings travel to Earth?

▶ With sextillions of stars in the universe, it is likely that other planets sustain intelligent life.

Are we there yet? Interstellar travel

The closest planet with intelligent life might be more than 20.2 light-years (117 trillion miles, or 189 trillion kilometers) away. Using our most advanced technology, it would still take us 761,000 years to reach this planet! Even if we could travel at the fastest speed possible—the speed of light (669,600,000 miles per hour, or 1,080,000,000 kilometers per hour)—it would still take over 20 years to arrive. Traveling to or from more distant planets could take millions of years. Given these vast distances, interplanetary travel seems unlikely, though not impossible.

▲ About 36 percent of Americans believe that UFOs exist, and 10 percent claim to have seen one.

The rare earth hypothesis

A mind-boggling number of conditions are necessary to create intelligent life. A planet needs to be the right distance from the Sun, the right size, and the right temperature. It must have liquid water, DNA, and nearby planets big enough to shield it from space junk. Given these complex requirements, some scientists believe it is highly unlikely that intelligent life exists elsewhere. If this "rare earth hypothesis" is true, then humans are alone in the universe. This would explain why we rarely bump into beings we cannot identify. But given the size of the universe, most scientists reject this hypothesis.

Fasten your seat belts

Could shortcuts allow beings to zip through the universe faster than we originally thought possible? Scientists have proposed some theories that a highly advanced civilization could perhaps put to use.

Wormholes

Draw a dot on one end of a piece of paper. Call this Earth. Now draw another dot near the other end of the paper. Call this Gliese 581c, a planet 20.2 light-years away. Measure how far the dots are from each other (for instance, 8 inches, or 20 centimeters). Now, pick up your paper and bend it so that the dots are closer together—maybe only 2 inches (5 centimeters) apart. You will notice a sort of tunnel between the two dots. Call this a wormhole. Using a wormhole, which is a possible shortcut through space and time, we could more quickly bridge the distance between two distant places.

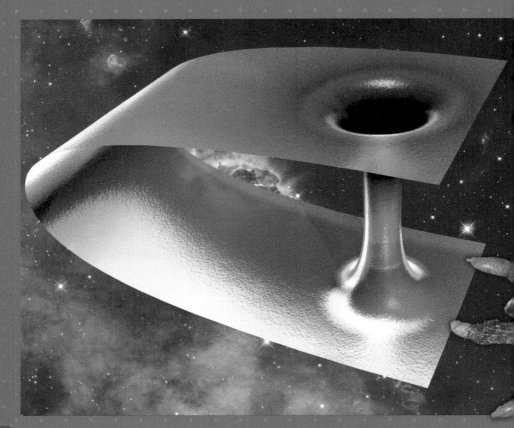

▲ If wormholes exist, they would make interplanetary travel faster and easier.

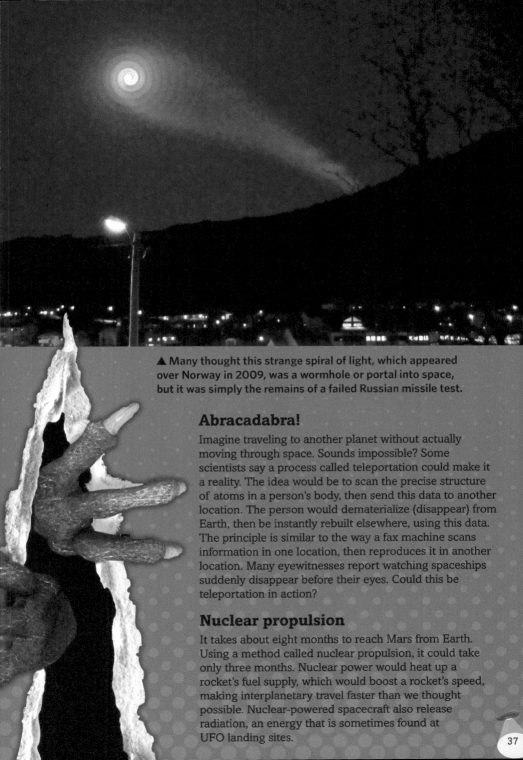

▲ Many thought this strange spiral of light, which appeared over Norway in 2009, was a wormhole or portal into space, but it was simply the remains of a failed Russian missile test.

Abracadabra!

Imagine traveling to another planet without actually moving through space. Sounds impossible? Some scientists say a process called teleportation could make it a reality. The idea would be to scan the precise structure of atoms in a person's body, then send this data to another location. The person would dematerialize (disappear) from Earth, then be instantly rebuilt elsewhere, using this data. The principle is similar to the way a fax machine scans information in one location, then reproduces it in another location. Many eyewitnesses report watching spaceships suddenly disappear before their eyes. Could this be teleportation in action?

Nuclear propulsion

It takes about eight months to reach Mars from Earth. Using a method called nuclear propulsion, it could take only three months. Nuclear power would heat up a rocket's fuel supply, which would boost a rocket's speed, making interplanetary travel faster than we thought possible. Nuclear-powered spacecraft also release radiation, an energy that is sometimes found at UFO landing sites.

Other theories

It is also possible that aliens are not extraterrestrials.
Perhaps they simply live in realms we do not understand.

Inter-dimensional hypothesis

We are aware of three dimensions: up-down, left-right,
and across. But mathematicians and physicists believe
that up to 11 other dimensions exist. This has led
some researchers to propose that aliens may exist in a
dimension on or near Earth that we simply cannot yet
see or understand. These beings might occasionally
"cross over" into our realm by controlling space and time.

▲ As Marty McFly
(Michael J. Fox, pictured
on the right) discovered in
the 1985 sci-fi movie *Back
to the Future*, traveling
back in time would be
problematic or even
impossible, since it would
change future events.

Future-nauts

Could aliens actually be...us? Some UFO-logists believe that aliens are future versions of humans, traveling back in time to visit their ancestors. After all, aliens do resemble humans more than other animals. However, traveling to the past is problematic. For instance, what if you went back to the past and killed your mother... before she had given birth to you? Does that mean that you would never exist? But some scientists get around this problem by suggesting that the universe breaks into parallel universes each time a different choice is made. In one universe, your mother is alive and well. In another one, she no longer exists. If aliens are future humans, perhaps they are trying to warn us to make more positive choices for the planet.

> "Time travel may be possible, but it is not practical."
>
> – Physicist Stephen Hawking

ET phone Earth?

Before trekking through space, wouldn't aliens simply give us a call? Many scientists think so, which is why they have developed a program called SETI (Search for Extraterrestrial Intelligence), where they send radio waves into the galaxy and listen for signals in return. Unfortunately, it could take over 2,000 years before we receive a response! Other scientists believe it is more likely that aliens would communicate telepathically (without using spoken or written language) or through writing. Many abductees have claimed telepathic communication with aliens.

▶ Like ET in the movie *ET*, many scientists believe that extraterrestrials would phone or send a message before traveling long distances through space.

Hallucinations and sleep paralysis

Do UFO sightings exist inside our heads, rather than in reality?

Hallucinations

Some researchers believe that UFO witnesses—especially abductees—are experiencing a type of hallucination, meaning that they are seeing, hearing, smelling, feeling, or tasting things that are not really there. Under hypnosis, abductees report images that are very similar to those reported by people experiencing hallucinations, as well as religious trances and near-death experiences. These people are probably experiencing something real, but the action may be occurring in their mind, rather than in the physical world.

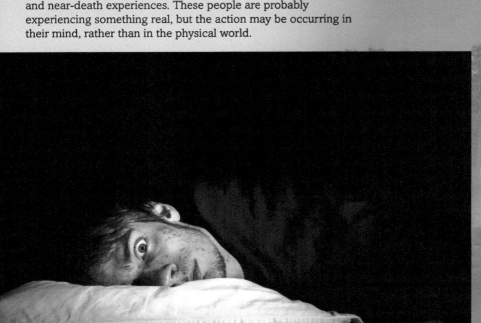

Sleep paralysis

When we dream, our bodies become temporarily paralyzed, so that we do not attempt to act out our dreams. But occasionally "sleep paralysis" occurs even when people are awake. This experience of being "frozen" can be terrifying, especially if the victim experiences a "sleep hallucination" at the same time. Sleep hallucination victims see vivid and sometimes scary images.

▲ Are people who report abduction experiences really experiencing sleep paralysis and sleep hallucinations instead?

In Australia, a couple saw a strange sight. They watched a person move his body as if he were meeting ETs and entering a spaceship. But the couple saw no aliens or spaceship. The person later gave a detailed account of an abduction experience. Was he hallucinating?

Hollywood images

Chances are, you have never seen an alien. But you probably have seen images of aliens in books, movies, and TV programs. These images may affect what we dream and remember. Just days before abductee Barney Hill (see page 14) underwent hypnosis, a science fiction program called *The Outer Limits* was shown on TV. During hypnosis, Hill sketched a picture of an alien that looked a lot like the one on the program. We do not know if Hill watched it, but we do know that many abductees describe very similar images.

▲ Images from television, books, movies, and magazines can influence how we understand unusual objects in "real life."

CAN THE MYSTERY BE SOLVED?

There is no reason to suppose that all UFO sightings have the same cause. Some people may have seen clouds, while others may have seen meteors or experimental aircraft. That would explain why the descriptions of UFOs have varied. But we cannot ignore the fact that a small percentage of UFO sightings appear to be objects that we truly cannot identify. And a number of alien abduction cases point to experiences we truly do not understand.

The final report

So far, no one has uncovered hard, physical evidence that cannot be produced by earthly means—no space helmet for a strange head, no crashed spaceship, no alien body, no unfamiliar high-tech devices, no unknown chemical samples. Until such evidence is available, it cannot be proved that UFOs are anything other than earthly objects. But the number and quality of unexplained UFO sightings and encounters offer reason for further investigation.

▼ Do aliens really exist? If so, might they look like this model of an alien?

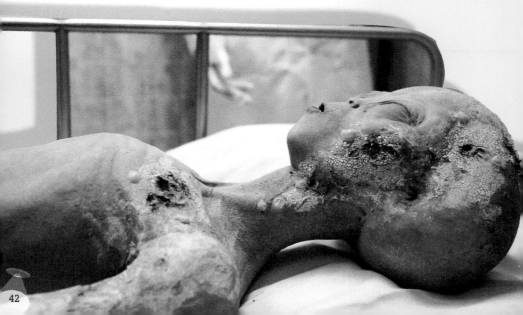

Is the truth out there?

For years, many government agencies investigated UFO sightings. But most of these records were kept secret. And some former federal investigators say that the government was more interested in finding quick explanations for sightings than in conducting complete and honest investigations.

A well-known U.S. study from 1968 called the Condon Report concluded that UFOs did not deserve further scientific study. Yet over 23 percent of the cases in the study were unsolved—and most had knowledgeable witnesses and strong evidence! After the report, many scientists who wanted to study UFOs weren't taken seriously, and many citizens who reported them were considered crazy.

▲ Are governments secretly investigating UFOs and aliens in top-secret areas? We may never know for sure.

Signs of openness

The U.S. Federal Bureau of Investigation (FBI) and government agencies in France and the United Kingdom recently released UFO records to the public. These documents show that most governments have taken UFO reports seriously. If the mystery of UFOs will ever be solved, scientists must have access to complete UFO data and be encouraged to investigate.

TIMELINE

11,000 BCE
An ancient Egyptian scroll describes residents throwing themselves to the ground in fear as they watch circles of fire in the sky

569 BCE
The prophet Ezekiel writes about a glowing metallic object in the skies

200 BCE–**600** CE
Animal and geometric patterns, which can only be seen from high above, are carved in the Nazca Desert in southern Peru

1300s
A fresco of the crucifixion shows a man traveling through the sky in an egg-shaped vehicle

1947
Pilot Kenneth Arnold encounters nine metallic objects skipping through the sky like saucers, in one of the first official UFO reports of the modern era

1947
An object crashes on a farmer's field near Roswell, New Mexico. The U.S. government first says it was a flying saucer, then a weather balloon, and then a top-secret type of balloon.

1950
Baseball team owner Nick Mariana films two UFOs floating over his stadium

1961
Betty and Barney Hill experience what they describe as an abduction into a spacecraft and claim they were given medical examinations

1961
Stephen Michalak experiences symptoms of radiation poisoning after an encounter with a UFO in the Canadian wilderness

1974
John and Susan Day and their family report being taken on board a spaceship by aliens and lectured about pollution

1976
The Iranian Air Force sends two fighter planes up to intercept a mysterious bright light. The craft escapes and appears to shut down communication and weapons systems on both planes.

1979
Swiss farmer Billy Meier electrifies the world with his tales of encounters with Pleiadians, later revealed to be false

1980
A mysterious pyramid-shaped object lands in Rendlesham Forest, near Bentwaters Air Force base in England

1989–1990
Thousands of residents witness brightly lit, flat, triangular objects in the skies over Belgium

1996
Movie producer Ray Santilli releases footage of an alien autopsy he claimed was filmed in 1947, after the Roswell crash. It is shown later that year on the Fox television network.

2006
Ray Santilli admits his alien autopsy footage was fake

2006
A disc-shaped craft hovers over a United Airlines gate at O'Hare Airport in Chicago for about 15 minutes before cutting a hole in the clouds

2012
Al-Ghad newspaper publishes a story about an alien invasion in Jafr, Jordan, leading to panic before readers learned it was an April Fools' Day joke

FITTING THE FACTS?

In some cases, governments appear to be hiding information or offering explanations that do not fit the facts.

Here are a couple of examples.

Who's fooling whom?

In 1947, a large object crashed on a farm near Roswell, New Mexico. At first, the U.S. military said the object was a flying saucer! Then it said it was a weather balloon. Almost 50 years later, it announced it was really a top-secret spy balloon. These changing stories—along with conflicting eyewitness accounts—have raised many questions about what really happened at Roswell.

Cutting a hole in the clouds

In 2006, over a dozen United Airlines employees reported seeing a disc-shaped object hover for several minutes over a gate at O'Hare Airport in Chicago. Then it shot up so fast that it cut a crisp hole in the clouds. The Federal Aviation Authority said the object was probably just a weather phenomenon called a punch-hole cloud. But meteorologists rejected this explanation. Is the government hiding the truth? Or is it simply not interested in finding an explanation?

Rumors and conspiracy theories

When governments withhold information, many people start filling in the blanks with rumors or made-up stories. For instance, many people believe that the U.S. government is keeping flying saucers and aliens in a restricted military zone called Area 51 in southern Nevada. Though we may never know exactly what happens in Area 51, it is more likely to involve building and testing top-secret military aircraft and other high-tech weapons than entertaining aliens.

GLOSSARY

altitude height of something, usually measured from above sea level

autopsy examination of a dead body to help find the cause of death

blimp large airship, usually used for observation

control tower building at an airport from which air traffic is observed and controlled

dematerialize disappear in physical form

electromagnetic field area consisting of both electric and magnetic forces, created by the presence of electricity in an electrical conductor

extraterrestrial occurring outside Earth; a being from outside Earth

Extraterrestrial Hypothesis hypothesis, or theory, that some UFOs are extraterrestrial life or aliens from other planets visiting Earth in spacecraft

flare device that produces a bright light, primarily used for signaling

hallucination experience of sensing something that is not really there

hypnosis state of mind resembling sleep in which the person is open to suggestion

hypnotist person who conducts hypnosis

hypothesis explanation for an occurrence or problem that needs evidence or testing before it can be accepted as true

infrared light type of light that is not visible to the human eye

interplanetary between planets

lenticular cloud still, lens-shaped cloud that forms at high altitudes

light-year distance that light can travel in one year (5.88 trillion miles, or 10 trillion kilometers)

missile object that is thrown or dropped on a target

near-death experience experience of being close to death, but surviving; often survivors see a white light

nuclear propulsion use of nuclear power to produce electricity or to heat the fuel that powers an engine

parallel universe hypothetical separate reality in which events unfold differently than those in the known universe

paralyzed unable to move voluntarily

physicist expert in the study of physics, the science of matter and energy

plateau area of raised ground

radar system for detecting the presence, direction, distance, and speed of aircraft and other objects by sending out radio waves

radiation poisoning illness from excessive exposure to radiation, resulting in a range of symptoms, from sickness and headache to loss of hair and teeth and even death

radioactive releasing radiation, an energy that travels through material or space

satellite device placed in orbit around Earth, the Moon, or another planet in order to gain information or communication

sleep hallucination hallucination that often occurs as a person is just falling asleep or just waking up

space junk collection of human-made objects orbiting Earth that no longer serve any useful purpose, such as old satellites

supersonic greater than the speed of sound

trance dreamlike state in which a person is unaware of his or her physical surroundings

weather balloon balloon used to carry instruments to gather weather data in the atmosphere

wormhole hypothetical connection between widely separated regions of space and time

FIND OUT MORE

BOOKS

Martin, Michael. *Alien Abductions* (Edge Books: The Unexplained). Mankato, Minn.: Capstone, 2006.

Mason, Paul. *Investigating UFOs and Aliens.* (Fact Finders: Extreme). Mankato, Minn.: Capstone, 2009.

Rooney, Anne. *UFOs and Aliens* (Amazing Mysteries). Mankato, Minn.: Smart Apple Media, 2010.

WEB SITES

You will find lots of great information about UFOs on the Internet. Just keep in mind that lots of people have strong views about UFOs, and some of these views have little or no basis in scientific fact. When browsing the Internet, make sure you note the source of the information and consider why the author might be presenting it. Here are a few recommended web sites:

www.kidskonnect.com/subject-index/15-science/107-ufo.html
This site contains fun UFO facts and links to web sites.

starchild.gsfc.nasa.gov/docs/StarChild/questions/question24.html
This NASA page explores how scientists search for alien life in the universe.

www.ufoevidence.org
This web site gives international evidence for UFOs, including sighting accounts, photos, physical evidence records, government reports and studies, physics studies and theories, as well as links to other resources.

MOVIES

Close Encounters of the Third Kind (Sony Pictures, 1977). After a man has a life-changing encounter with a UFO, he meets others who have had similar "visions," as well as government researchers who believe that aliens are preparing to make contact with humans.

Contact (Warner Brothers, 1997). When a radio astronomer discovers Earth's first extraterrestrial radio signal, she must decide what it means.

Fire in the Sky (Paramount, 1993). This is based on the real-life 1975 account of Travis Walton, a logger who encountered a huge UFO with his friends. His friends fled, but Travis was missing for several days and claims he was abducted.

UFOs and Aliens (New Video, 2011). This History Channel special explores different stories about UFOs and aliens in depth.

UFOs: The Secret History (UFO TV, 2010). Find out about the origins of the UFO phenomenon and the Extraterrestrial Hypothesis.

TOPICS TO RESEARCH

• What are some ways to tell if a UFO photo is fake?

• Sightings of black triangles, like the Belgian triangle, have been on the rise in recent years. What are some theories for what these objects could be?

INDEX